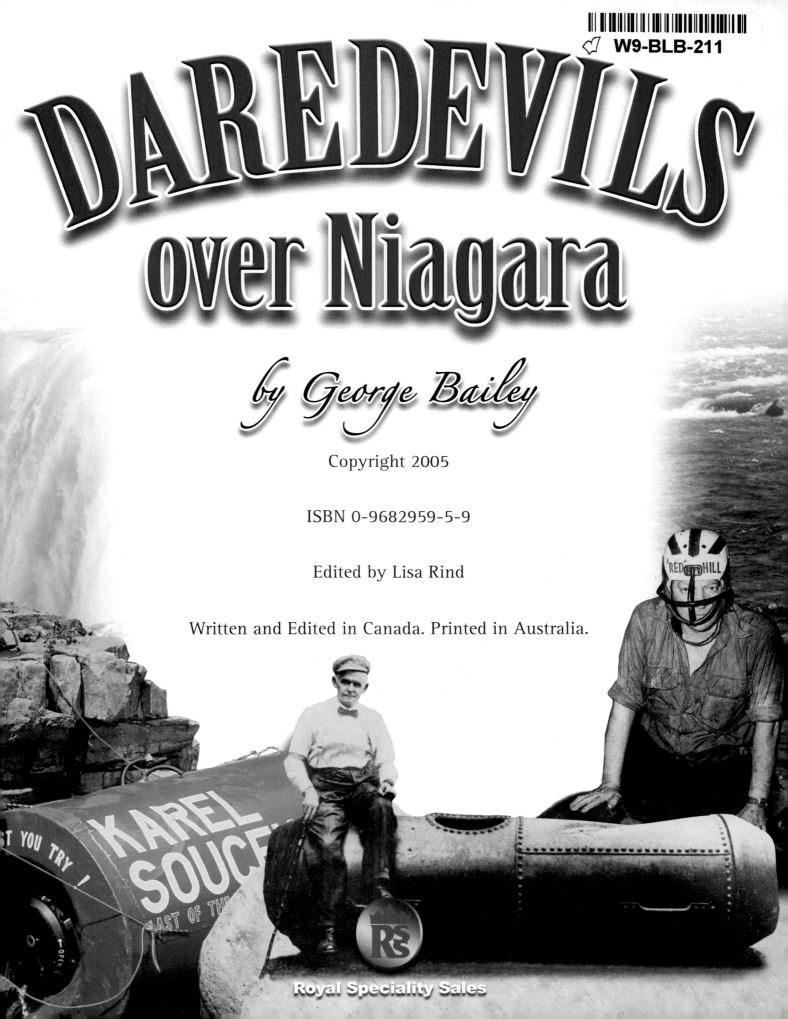

DAREDEVILS
over Niagara

by George Bailey

Copyright 2005

ISBN 0-9682959-5-9

Edited by Lisa Rind

Written and Edited in Canada. Printed in Australia.

Royal Speciality Sales

DAREDEVILS over Niagara

❧ CONTENTS ❧

Prologue

Between October 24, 1901, and October 20, 2003, 16 different people, including two women, have intentionally tried to "beat" Niagara by plunging over the Canadian Horseshoe Falls. Two of these people went over twice, while two other people went over the Falls at the same time in the same barrel. All but one did it with the aid of some type of barrel or device. Five of these people lost their lives in the attempt.

Like the barrels themselves, their reasons for doing so were all different. For some, it was the hope of instant fame or fortune, and for others it was simply a personal challenge.

Here now are the stories of those Niagara daredevils.

DAREDEVIL No. 1
Annie Edson Taylor, October 24, 1901: Survived

The first person to get the barrel rolling was Annie Edson Taylor, a 63-year-old former school teacher from Bay City, Michigan. The impoverished widow came to Niagara in September 1901, determined to do a single deed of daring to solve her economic problems. Taylor announced that she intended to go over the Canadian Horseshoe Falls in a barrel and on October, 1901, she kept her promise.

The contrivance in which she proposed to make the trip was a Kentucky oak barrel which was five and a half feet tall, three feet in diameter through the middle, 15 inches at the base and 28 inches at the head. The device was bound with seven iron hoops. The opening where Taylor was to enter the barrel measured 14 inches by 10 inches and was closed with a fastener of heavy oak and iron clasps. The barrel was not painted and resembled a conga drum. Inside, it was fitted with a harness into which Taylor strapped herself. Two large cushions protected her. In front of her face were three small air holes fitted with corks and a short piece of rubber hose which she held in her mouth.

There were concerns by those who helped her that she would be killed during her stunt. In order to allay these concerns, she agreed to float the barrel over the Falls first with a cat in it. The barrel survived, but the cat perished!

Taylor refused to be disheartened and returned the barrel to the carpenter for minor repairs. Once completed, she was ready to go.

After having postponed her trip twice in one week due to strong winds, she announced she was ready on Thursday, October 24, 1901.

Two men who were hired to assist Taylor rowed her and the barrel to Grass Island on the American side of the Niagara River about a mile above the Falls.

Taylor was then helped into the barrel. The assistants screwed on the lid, pumped air into the barrel with a bicycle pump and then rolled her into the water. They towed it towards the Canadian Horseshoe Falls and at 4:05 p.m., the barrel was cut loose for its journey down the Niagara River. She would later say: "I prayed every second, except after the fall when I was unconscious. Nobody ought to ever do that again!"

Annie Edson Taylor
Oct. 24, 1901

At 4:23 p.m., the barrel made its plunge and in less than 30 seconds, it was seen in the waters below the Falls in the area locals call the "shoe". The barrel was carried swiftly down to the green water halfway to the Maid of the Mist eddy, where helpers with a pole and hook drew it towards the rocks. At 4:40 p.m., the barrel was secured by spectators, one of them being Mark Munday. (The "Munday" name would appear many years later in connection with other barrel rides over the Falls.)

In no time the cover was removed and the news was shouted that the woman was alive.

It was not so easy to get Taylor out of the barrel though. First, a saw and wrench had to be obtained to enlarge the opening. Lifted from the barrel, Taylor waved feebly and thanked God she was alive.

Miraculously, Taylor suffered only minor injuries - a gash to her scalp, a mild concussion and nervous shock. Unhappily, Taylor's dream to be free of financial worries did not happen. The self-titled "Queen of the Mist" was not much of a promoter and within a year she was back in Niagara after an unsuccessful vaudeville tour, poorer than when she left!

A similar wooden barrel (since someone stole her original one) was put on display in a Niagara Falls museum. She died at the age of 83, penniless, in the Niagara County Hospital in Lockport, New York. Since she didn't have enough money to pay for a burial, some of her admirers chipped in. She was laid to rest at Oakwood Cemetery in Niagara Falls, New York.

DAREDEVIL No. 2
Bobby Leach, July 25, 1911: Survived

For a decade, everyone followed Taylor's advice: "Nobody ought to ever do that again".

However, there was one Niagara resident of Cockney origin named Bobby Leach who maintained that anything Annie could do, he could do better. Leach operated a restaurant at the foot of Bridge Street in Niagara Falls and repeatedly boasted to visitors that he would make the trip over the Falls. He made good on his promise on July 25, 1911.

Leach's barrel was made of steel, cylindrical in shape and floated horizontally. In mid-afternoon, his barrel was shoved into the Niagara River near the entrance to the Welland River (at Chippawa Creek). Shortly after 3 p.m., his vessel went over the Falls in one piece. However, it was not until 20 minutes later that the barrel was secured by an Ontario

BOBBY LEACH and his Barrel after his perilous trip over Niagara Falls, July 25th, 1911
Copyright 1911. U.S.A. & CANADA by Bobby Leach.

Power Plant employee who tied a rope around it after he jumped into the river. By the time the 54-year-old stunter was dragged out, his jaw and both kneecaps had been smashed. He spent six months in the hospital recuperating from his injuries.

Leach was relatively successful in capitalizing on his trip by exhibiting his barrel at vaudeville theatres and lecture halls in the United States, Canada and England. He also made a film about his trip over the Falls.

Unfortunately, during a later tour of New Zealand with his wife and young daughter, he slipped on an orange peel, fell to the sidewalk and broke his leg. The limb became infected and during an operation to amputate it, Leach died of shock. He was buried in April, 1926, in Hillboro Cemetery in Auckland, New Zealand, at the age of 69.

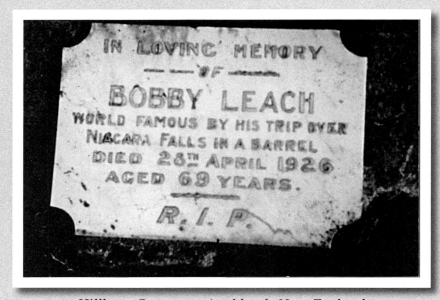

Hillboro Cemetery, Auckland, New Zealand

DAREDEVIL No. 3

Charles G. Stephens, July 11, 1920: Drowned

The third person to attempt to conquer Niagara was also from England and his name was Charles G. Stephens. Stephens was a barber from Bristol, England, with a family of 11 children. His previous experience as a stunter included jumping from an airplane with a parachute and putting his head in the mouths of lions.

"There is no secret about the reason for my plunge", said Stephens. "I want the money. I don't like the barbering business".

Stephens made the perilous trip in a heavy wooden barrel on July 11, 1920. He began his journey at approximately 8:10 a.m. at a point about three miles above the Falls on the American side. After he travelled over the Falls, thousands saw the wooden craft break into pieces as it hit the base of the Canadian Horseshoe Falls. The 58-year-old stunter made one big mistake in the construction of his barrel - he had secured a 100-pound anvil, the ballast for his barrel, to his feet. The only remains found was Stephens' right arm, recognizable by its tattoos and still harnessed to the wreckage of the craft.

It is generally believed that his torso went to the bottom of the river attached to the anvil. Niagara Falls had claimed its first Falls daredevil. Others were to follow.

Jean Albert Lussier, July 4, 1928: Survived

Jean Albert Lussier of Springfield, Massachussetts, chose July 4, 1928, to go over Niagara Falls in a barrel. Lussier, a 36-year-old machinist, made the trip without suffering so much as a scratch.

At a cost of $1,585, Lussier designed and built a 758-pound orange rubber ball. It was six feet in diameter with an outer and inner framework of steel bands, covered with canvas and lined with 32 inflated inner tubes. A 100-pound weight acted as ballast. The design was similar to another barrel that would eventually make the trip in 1961.

After a race with police, who attempted to stop Lussier from entering the river, he successfully launched his craft five miles above the Falls. With about 2,000 spectators lining both sides of the river, Lussier was swept downstream at about 3:20 p.m. and over the Falls about five minutes later. He was the first person to go over the Falls in an inflated contraption. Although caught for about a minute in the "shoe", the area directly below the Horseshoe Falls, Lussier was eventually thrown out by the current and swept downriver. A small boat launched from the Maid of the Mist dock caught and towed the ball to shore.

During a later description, Lussier said: "The trip was nothing. She feels like a smooth, easy, ski jump". Future riders would describe their successful rides in a similar manner.

Lussier was relatively successful in capitalizing on his trip. Lussier moved to Niagara Falls, New York, and for several years, he sold pieces of the rubber tubing of his inner lining for fifty cents a cut. Some will tell you he must have had hundreds of tubes in that barrel!

Lussier talked, like other stunters who were to follow, about going over the American Falls in a barrel, but never did.

He died in 1971 in Niagara Falls, New York.

DAREDEVIL No. 5
George A. Stathakis, July 5, 1930: Suffocated

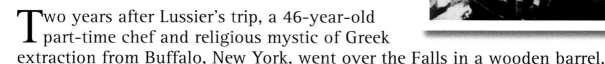

Two years after Lussier's trip, a 46-year-old part-time chef and religious mystic of Greek extraction from Buffalo, New York, went over the Falls in a wooden barrel.

The fondest companion of this bachelor was his turtle named Sonny, whom he believed to be more than 105 years old. Sonny was to join Stathakis on his trip over the Falls.

Stathakis revealed that going over the Falls was part of his lifelong search for truth. His barrel was the heaviest to date, weighing 1,000 pounds. It was 10 feet tall, five feet in diameter and fitted with iron bumpers on the top and bottom. Stathakis paid a cooperage company $400 to make his device.

A mattress was stowed in the barrel for comfort, a pencil and a notebook to record his impressions, an oxygen tank with three hours of air supply, and the pet turtle Sonny.

Again, thousands of people lined both sides of the gorge to view Stathakis' trip. His barrel was towed from a boathouse to Navy Island in the upper Niagara River, then towed downriver to the head of the rapids at Chippawa. At 3:25 p.m., the tow line was cut.

Unfortunately, his barrel would not be spotted for another 18 hours. It was held captive by the wall of water behind the Falls. A boat towed the barrel to shore the next day. Ironically, some of the last words spoken by Stathakis to his helpers were: "If I don't come up in three hours, there won't be any use in living". He was right. According to Dr. W.W. Thompson, medical examiner of Niagara Falls, Stathakis suffocated.

When taken from the barrel, there was hardly a bruise on his body.

The notebook carried no record of his thoughts. There was considerable water in the barrel but there was no water in the lungs of the dead man. Sonny the turtle, however, survived.

The chef's body lay in the county morgue for someone to claim, but no one ever did.

Niagara had claimed its second victim. The third would be taken 21 years later.

DAREDEVIL No. 6
William (Red) Hill Jr., August 5, 1951: Drowned

It was on August 5, 1951, that William (Red) Hill Jr., son of the famous "Niagara River Master" Red Hill Sr., chose to go over the Falls. He was to travel in a flimsy rubber contraption made of 13 inner tire tubes held together by webbing and canvas. He called it "The Thing".

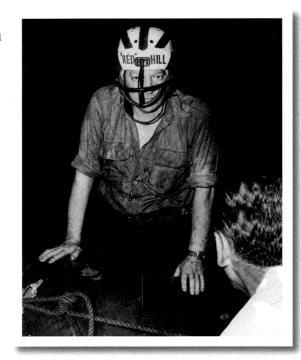

At 2:30 p.m., the 38-year-old stunter set out on his journey after being towed into the Niagara River at Ussher's Creek Bridge, a few miles above the Falls on the Canadian side. The stunt was well publicized and thousands lined the banks to watch.

The Thing had a rough trip through the upper rapids, before going over the Falls at about 3 p.m. All that emerged was a tangle of inner tubes and torn netting. Hill was nowhere in sight. What remained of "The Thing" was reached by a small boat launched from the Maid of the Mist dock by Hill's brother Norman "Corky". When he reached the contraption, he wept and exclaimed: "There's nobody in it"! The only thing found in the contraption was his brother's shoe. The red mattress Hill had rested on surfaced the next day.

The Niagara River relinquished its third daredevil victim the following morning, near the Canadian shore. Hill had drowned.

Following Hill's death, there was considerable public indignation, causing Ontario's then-Premier, Leslie Frost, to issue a special order. In future, The Niagara Parks Commission, an agency of the Ontario government, would arrest not only those attempting such a stunt, but also those who assisted. Under the Niagara Parks Act, it became an offence to perform a stunt without the permission of the Commission. Since that day, no such permission has ever been granted. A similar law exists on the American side of the border.

DAREDEVIL No. 7
William FitzGerald (AKA Nathan Boya), July 15, 1961: Survived

Thirty -year-old William A. FitzGerald of New York City plunged over Niagara Falls in a barrel or ball similar to the type Jean Lussier used. The 1,200 pound black ball was six feet in diameter, with a 16-gauge steel frame and covered with light gauge cage-like metal sprayed with a rubber-like substance. Inflated cushions were wedged into the hollow between the inner and outer chambers to add buoyancy.

At 10:56 a.m., FitzGerald plunged over the Canadian Horseshoe Falls. In deep contrast to his predecessors, he made the plunge unannounced and with no fanfare. The craft performed extremely well and the Niagara Parks Police had no difficulty rowing out to meet it. The quiet daredevil was easily arrested.

FitzGerald's vessel came to be known as the "Plunge-O-Sphere" because inside was a banner that read: "Plunge-O-Sphere from your pit of darkness into light dell". The words and the man remain a mystery to this day.

After his successful trip, which FitzGerald did "for very, very personal reasons", the stunter became the first person to be charged under the Niagara Parks Act for performing a stunt on Commission lands without the permission of The Niagara Parks Commission. For this deed, he was fined $100 plus $13 court costs.

In 1962, FitzGerald wrote about his trip in an article in Science and Mechanics magazine. "I clawed overhead for the grip with which I could hold to try to hold the top closed by hand, just as the sphere was swept over the brink. Down we went, the sphere and I, deep into the violence of the lower basin. Before the Sphere's 5,000 pounds of lift could reverse the dive, savage forces ripped the hatch grip from my hand. Soon, it flapped back on its welded hinge. Driving spray shot through into the capsule, threatening a watery grave. But Niagara was cheated of her victim. Carried by swift currents, the sphere burst out of the vapour shroud into the bright sunlight. I unbuckled the belts and gave her a few pats".

Today, we know FitzGerald has made several trips to Niagara since 1961. He visited Niagara Falls in 1984 for the funeral of daredevil Karel Soucek. FitzGerald later earned a doctorate in sociology and did post-doctoral training as a medical behavioural scientist. At one time, he was a faculty fellow at a medical school in New York City.

William FitzGerald along with a police officer, examines the inside of this ball.

DAREDEVIL No. 8
Karel Soucek, July 2, 1984: Survived

Twenty-three years were to pass before the cry was once more shouted: "There's a barrel in the water and it's headed for the Falls!"

This time, the barrel contained a professional stuntman from Hamilton, Ontario, Karel Soucek. Soucek was a small man who made a living as the manager and promoter of a speedway in Hamilton, where he jumped motorcycles over cars and house trailers and even crashed an airplane into a barn. The 37-year-old Czech-born stunter was not unknown to the Niagara Parks Police. On July 22, 1976, Soucek had attempted to cross the Whirlpool Rapids on a moped using the lines of the Niagara Spanish Aero Car attraction. The attempt failed. Soucek had travelled 20 feet when his moped hit a metal bolt on the cable and he was derailed. A safety harness prevented a fall.

The barrel in which Soucek chose to make his 9:30 a.m. trip over the Falls on July 2, 1984, was shaped like a cigar butt, with an outer frame made of transparent plastic. Soucek carried a two-way radio and sat on an inflatable bucket seat wearing a safety harness. He entered the 500-pound barrel through a sealed hatch that locked from inside and out. The cost of the barrel was about $3,000.

Soucek was the first barrel rider to enter the Niagara River just 164 yards above the Horseshoe Falls. Early that morning, a cube van backed up to the retaining wall above the Falls and a crew of four pulled out a plywood ramp, leaned it against the wall and slid the barrel into the river. It took about 30 seconds for Soucek to become the eighth person to go over Niagara Falls in a contraption and the

The ramp rests on the parapet above the Falls.
Photo - G. Bailey

Spectators watch as the barrel enters the Niagara River above the Falls.

fifth to survive the attempt.

After the plunge, the vessel appeared only slightly damaged. Soucek was in good shape, with the exception of a slight cut on his forehead. He refused to clean the cut until reporters had a chance to photograph him.

After the barrel was released, the crew feverishly headed to the Table Rock Scenic Tunnels (now the Journey Behind the Falls), paid their admission fee (the cashier had no idea what was happening) and took the elevator to the base of the Falls. Forty-five minutes later they retrieved their hero from the barrel. From there, escorted by Niagara Parks Police, Soucek was taken to Greater Niagara General Hospital and given a clean bill of health. Later that day, the barrel was dislodged. It had floated down river where it was retrieved by a crew from the Maid of the Mist.

Soucek had hoped to become wealthy within a year of the stunt. He had prepared well for his feat and not only had he made arrangements for the video taping of his ride, but he also had media kits waiting for eager reporters at a media conference he called for later in the afternoon.

On July 11, 1984, Soucek appeared at the Niagara Falls Provincial Courthouse where he was fined $500 plus court costs for an offence under The Niagara Parks Act, which prohibits stunting without the written permission of The Niagara Parks Commission.

Soucek's barrel is caught in the eddy below the Falls and finally secured by Niagara Parks Police.
Photos - G. Bailey

Sadly, Soucek was not to become wealthy and within six months, he was dead as a result of a stunt in the Houston Astrodome in Texas. Attempting to duplicate his Falls plunge before an audience of 35,000 people, a specially designed wooden barrel was pushed off a 180-foot platform into a 10-foot pool of water. The barrel hit the edge of the pool and Soucek died January 20, 1985, of injuries suffered in the plunge.

Karel Soucek was buried in the Drummond Hill Cemetery in Niagara Falls, in a plot donated by Ken Sloggett, a relative of a former Niagara daredevil, William (Red) Hill, Jr. Former Niagara Falls daredevil, William FitzGerald attended the funeral to pay his respects.

Inside Soucek's barrel.

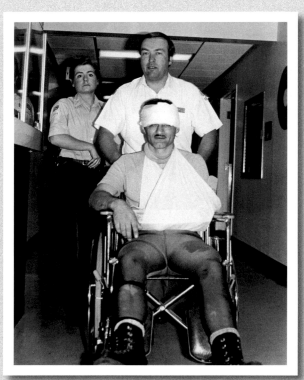

Soucek is wheeled into the Greater Niagara General Hospital by paramedics.
Photo - G. Bailey

DAREDEVIL No. 9
Steven Trotter, August 18, 1985: Survived

A brash, likeable 22-year-old would-be stuntman from Fort Lauderdale, Florida, was the next to challenge the Falls and win.

Steven Trotter, a bachelor originally from Barrington, Rhode Island, tumbled over the Canadian Horseshoe Falls after entering the Niagara River from Goat Island on the American Side of the border on Sunday, August 18, 1985.

This was not the first time Trotter had attempted a stunt. On November 12, 1984, he was prevented from launching a barrel from the Canadian side of the border by the Niagara Parks Police.

Steven Trotter's barrel, which he referred to as "The Rig", was homemade and consisted of eight tractor-trailer inner tubes surrounding a fiberglass capsule. It was 15 feet long and six feet in diameter. Inside the capsule, which was lined with thick foam similar to that which is used as nuclear warhead packing, were two air tanks, a two-way radio and an underwater flashlight. Trotter estimated the cost of his barrel at $6,200 US.

The inner tubes were covered with a dark green tarpaulin with names and advertising written on it. On one side, "Support Reagan" appeared in large red, white and blue lettering. Then-U.S. President Ronald Reagan was one of Trotter's favourite people. The entire trip over the Falls lasted less than a minute. On impact, two of the large inner tubes deflated and a big dent was made in the

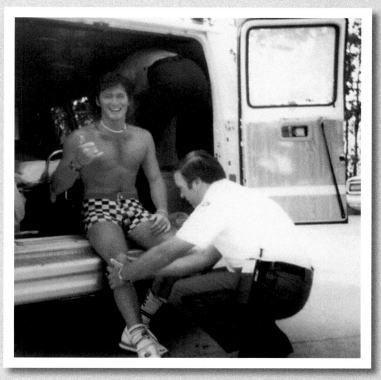

Trotter "hams it up" after his successful trip.
Photos - G. Bailey

inner capsule. The hatch was blown off, but luckily the vessel remained afloat and Trotter managed to climb out of the inner shell, jump into the water and float alongside, waving to spectators. A crew from the Maid of the Mist picked him up uninjured.

On shore, he was in great spirits and shouted several times: "I made it! I made it!" After being given a clean bill of health, Trotter returned to the Maid of the Mist landing to sign autographs and be photographed by spectators.

Later that day during a media conference, Trotter said the trip was "cool ... like dropping in an elevator without a cable".

Steven Trotter was later charged under the Niagara Parks Act for performing a stunt without the written permission of The Niagara Parks Commission and fined $500 plus court costs. Trotter was later fined another $5,000 by the U.S. Coast guard for violating a safety zone in the Niagara River.

Steven Trotter's name reappears later in this book. He appeared in court with John "Dave" Munday, who was charged with attempting to perform a stunt by going over the Falls in a barrel on July 28, 1985. His barrel ran aground in the upper Niagara River after Ontario Hydro lowered the water in the retaining pool to thwart the stunt. Munday was fined $500, placed on probation, and warned not to attempt the stunt again. He did not take the advice seriously.

Photo - G. Bailey

DAREDEVIL No. 10
John "Dave" Munday, October 5, 1985: Survived

John Munday, known as Dave, was a 48-year-old diesel mechanic from Caistor Centre, Ontario. The stunter had a 20-year-old obsession to plunge over the Falls in a barrel. The mechanic and skydiving instructor chose a flexible barrel that was designed not to sink.

Munday's plastic and aluminum barrel was six feet by five feet and was equipped with a two-way radio and a video camera that taped the event through a porthole.

Munday went over the Canadian Horseshoe Falls on Saturday, October 5, 1985.

The Munday barrel was launched near the same location used by Soucek in 1984. After backing a van containing the barrel up to the retaining wall, a ramp was pulled out and a six-member crew slid the craft over the retaining wall into the river, about 328 feet from the brink. It is reported that the crew had a difficult time lifting the barrel over the wall and a number of tourists came to their aid.

The barrel crashed over the cataract in seconds, only to become tangled in the currents directly below in the "shoe". It was lodged just below the Table Rock Scenic Tunnel attraction (now called Journey Behind the Falls).

Crew members paid their way into the attraction and went to the plaza level below the Falls. Munday's crew was

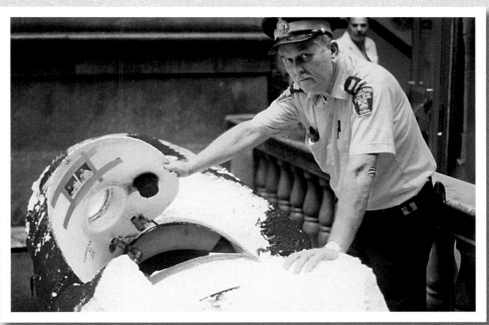

Photo - G. Bailey

Munday is interviewed from below the Falls after his successful trip.   Photo - M. Bailey

17

in constant contact with him and it was learned immediately that he was uninjured. It was difficult to capture the barrel with the cold, heavy mist driving into their faces. Finally, crew member Ken Sloggett dove into the treacherous river with a rope tied around his waist to retrieve the craft from the current. Thanks to Sloggett, Munday was freed from his 750-pound red and silver barrel just 45 minutes after the drop.

Newspaper and radio media and approximately twenty tourists, along with the Parks Police, were waiting to greet Munday when he stepped over the retaining wall below the Falls at the edge of the attraction.

Escorted to the top of the Falls by elevator, he was welcomed by hundreds of spectators who had gathered at the exit of the attraction. Cries of "Way to go, Dave!" could be heard. The quiet stunter refused medical treatment and was whisked away to the Niagara Parks police station where he was charged with two offences: unlawfully performing a stunt in the Niagara Parks and not complying with an earlier probation order.

The barrel was later retrieved from the lower Niagara River along with the video tape. Appearing later in Niagara Falls Provincial Court before the same judge who had earlier placed him on probation, he was fined $500 for performing the illegal stunt and an additional $1,000 for breach of probation.

After paying his fine, Munday quietly left the courtroom. He was no doubt satisfied that he had fulfilled a childhood dream and that the events were behind him. Or were they?

Ken Sloggett talks to the media about his treacherous dive into the lower Niagara River to rescue Munday.   Photo - G. Bailey

Photo - M. Bailey

DAREDEVILS No. 11
Jeffrey (Clyde) Petkovich and Peter DeBernardi, September 27, 1989: Survived

A new chapter in the history of Niagara Falls daredevils was written on September 27, 1989, when 24-year-old Jeffrey Petkovich and 42-year-old Peter DeBernardi became the first two person team to plunge over the Falls in the same barrel.

Both were natives of Niagara Falls. Petkovich was a psychology student at Carleton University in Ottawa and DeBernardi was an unemployed former race car driver.

The daring duo strapped themselves head-to-head in a yellow homemade steel barrel weighing one tonne called, "The Spirit of Niagara". Both men wore crash helmets with oxygen tanks and mouthpieces when they made their plunge.

A truck was driven to the parapet at the edge of the river and a 15-person crew rolled the barrel over the railing on a pipe and dolly system. They entered the Niagara River less than a mile from the brink. It took about 25 seconds before it crashed over the Falls. DeBernardi said later, "the barrel hit three boulders on the way down, but the landing was smooth and we popped up like a cork. The barrel did its job".

Both men suffered fat lips because of the mouthpieces attached to their oxygen tanks and a few minor bumps and bruises. Petkovich described the ride as: "… a smooth roller-coaster ride, a real free-fall with an abrupt halt".

The barrel drifted in eddies in the river for about 45 minutes, with both men listening to prepared stereo tapes: "Riverboat Fantasy" by David Wilcox and "The River" by Bruce Springsteen. Eventually the vessel floated close to the base of the Canadian Falls where it was snagged by a crew member with grappling hooks. Both parties emerged and were charged.

DeBernardi said he had gone through two partners before Petkovich. The two met just eight weeks before the trip, although DeBernardi had been planning the stunt for a year and a half. He was later quoted as saying he wanted to bring attention to the problem of drug addiction: "Knowing the safety standards we used for this plunge, we wanted to show the youth of today our chances of survival were way greater than theirs with a life of drugs".

Each was fined $1,500 for performing an illegal stunt. DeBernardi was fined an additional $500 because he had been warned not to perform the stunt. DeBernadi is quoted as saying that his fine was "a cheap price to pay to get into the history books".

In order to discourage future stunters, the Attorney General of Ontario introduced legislation to increase the fine for Falls stunters to a maximum of $10,000. Most importantly, the courts were also given the discretion to confiscate the daredevils' barrels. However, this still would not stop others in the future from making the plunge.

DAREDEVIL No. 12
Jessie Sharp, June 5, 1990: Died

Jessie Sharp was so sure he would survive a trip over Niagara Falls that he left his vehicle downstream at Lewiston, New York, and made dinner reservations. The 28-year-old Sharp of Ocoee, Tennessee, took the plunge on June 5, 1990, in a specially built red polyethylene kayak equipped with airbags. Inscribed on the side of the craft was the word "Rapidman". He was not wearing a helmet so that his face could be videotaped.

Sharp was naked to the waist and wore no life jacket, fearing it would restrict his ability to escape in the event that he got caught underneath the Falls. He was first spotted in the upper Niagara River by workers at the Ontario Hydro Control Structure. The workers began to close the gates to reduce the flow of water over the Falls in an effort to run the man aground. Video taped footage later showed Sharp effortlessly darting between the rocks jutting from the water above the Falls. At about 1:50 p.m., Sharp hit the cataract, raising his paddle over his head in a sign of triumph.

Sharp had hidden the kayak the day before along the Canadian shoreline about 1,000 yards south of the former Toronto Power Plant. He was described as an experienced kayaker and rafter and had been training for the ride for the past two years. His friends insisted that this was not a stunt for Sharp, it was simply a quest. He was an adventurer who wanted to fulfill a dream. Sharp had first attempted to go over the American Falls in 1980, but was stopped by U.S. authorities.

The kayak surfaced and was recovered at about 3 p.m. below the Falls, without Sharp. Apart from a small dent, it was unscathed.

Sharp became the 13th person to go over Niagara Falls intentionally. It was a number that proved unlucky as his body was never recovered.

Some people believe Sharp's ride over Niagara Falls could have been successful had the water been flowing at its full force. This could possibly have thrown him clear of the rocks below the Falls.

However, at any given time, 100,000 cubic feet of water per second (about half its potential flow) is diverted for power purposes.

DAREDEVIL No. 13
John (Dave) Munday (for a second time), September 26, 1993: Survived

At 8:35 a.m. on Sunday, September 28, 1993, 56 year-old Dave Munday of Caistor Centre, Ontario, became the only person to go over Niagara Falls twice and live to tell about it.

This time he spent $500 to convert a used Canadian Coast Guard 660-pound diving bell, with a 14-inch hatch, into a daredevil's vessel. The bell was ballasted with 200 pounds of sand and was painted red and white with a Canadian Maple Leaf. Words on the outside read: "David Munday challenges Niagara for the last time".

The vessel was equipped with a small supply of oxygen and contained about two inches of padding, two air valves, a snorkel-type breathing tube, a five-point auto racing harness and a neck strap. Airline sickness bags were fastened to the wall. There was no video camera on board. Compared to his previous barrel, this barrel could be described as no-frills.

Munday had a walkie-talkie taped to his left upper arm. He had also taped both lower arms "to keep them from breaking" and was wearing the same pair of "lucky" running shoes that he had worn on his first trip over Niagara. A bright yellow flotation vest completed his stunter's apparel.

The bell was rolled down a ramp from the back of a

Photo - M. Bailey

Photo - M. Bailey

flatbed truck into the Niagara River above the Canadian Horseshoe Falls from the same spot from which other barrels had been released. It was swept 300 yards to the cataract and within seconds, had crashed over the edge.

Munday was alive inside the barrel but sick and too weak to open the hatch. The small workboat called the Little Maid was deployed from the Maid of the Mist dock and just after 9 a.m., the barrel was captured and towed back to the dock.

Photo - M. Bailey

After Munday was able to muster up the strength, he opened the hatch but stayed in the barrel for about 10 minutes. At 9:33 a.m., friends lifted the pale, sick stunter from his barrel. Munday had no visible cuts and refused to go to the hospital. He was charged under the Trespass to Property Act and also under the Niagara Parks Act with stunting on Niagara Parks land without permission.

When Munday appeared in court in December, he was fined $6,000 for his second barrel ride over Niagara. In court, Munday told reporters he did not perform the stunt for profit. He said he was simply drawn by the power of Niagara Falls.

Photo - M. Bailey

DAREDEVILS No. 14
Steven Trotter (his second trip) and Lori Martin, June 18, 1995: Survived

A first for Niagara took place on Father's Day, June 18, 1995, at about 9:30 a.m.

Two people, 33-year-old Steve Trotter, a bartender from Fort Lauderdale, Florida and 29-year-old Lori Martin, a catering manager from Columbus, Georgia, became the first male-female pair to go over the Canadian Horseshoe Falls together. For Trotter, it was his second trip, having first conquered the cataract in 1985. Martin became the second woman to take the plunge since Annie Edson Taylor got the barrel rolling in 1901.

Their chosen vessel was white, 10 feet in length and weighed 1,100 pounds. Its high-tech properties, including a video camera attached to one end, cost the pair US$26,000.

A seven-member crew launched the airtight barrel from the back of a rental truck over the parapet about 100 yards above the Falls. Unfortunately, the end piece containing the video camera broke off during the launch.

Within seconds of entering the water the pair had made the plunge.

Limping, but smiling, it was about an hour later when the daring duo emerged from the barrel just below the Falls.

After exiting the barrel, Trotter and Martin were brought out of the gorge on stretchers and taken to Greater Niagara General Hospital by ambulance. Trotter is quoted as saying: "It was harder this time. It's the second and the last time around". The pair were treated for shock and numerous bumps.

Lori Martin (top) and Steven Trotter (middle) are rescued by emergency personnel below the Falls.

The battered barrel was retrieved eight days later when a crane lifted it from the algae-covered rocks below. Painted on the outside were the words, "The Cowboys from Hell" and "Take the Real Plunge." The retrieval had cost thousands of dollars.

The two were charged with trespassing, performing a stunt without a permit and mischief. When they appeared later in an Ontario court, Trotter was fined $5,000 after pleading guilty to a charge of stunting. He was also ordered to pay hospital costs of $515. Friends helped him raise money for the fine by selling T-shirts, at $15 each, bearing the message, "Take the Real Dive, Fall 95". Martin was released on $2,500 bail and given a court date for trial. The barrel remained in the possession of the Niagara Parks Police, who had put a lien against it to recoup the $2,200 recovery cost. The Niagara Falls Fire Department estimated the rescue had cost them $2,400 for the extra crew and The Niagara Parks Commission estimated it lost $2,200 while the Journey Behind the Falls attraction was closed.

Trotter, after paying the levied costs, returned to Niagara in August to reclaim his barrel.

All photos - M. Bailey

DAREDEVIL No. 15
Robert Overacker, October 1, 1995: Died

At about 12:35 p.m. on Sunday, October 1, 1995, a quiet 39-year-old man from Camarillo, California, jet-skied to his death over the Canadian Horseshoe Falls.

Robert "Firecracker" Overacker was trying to bring attention to the homeless in his home state of California. Overacker and two other men were spotted launching a blue Kawasaki jet ski into the upper Niagara River, less than a mile from the brink of the Falls. Once in the river, Overacker jumped on the vessel and drove out into the upper Niagara River. The stunter carried a walkie-talkie and wore a life jacket, a helmet spangled with stars, red Nike shoes, white gloves and a blue wet suit.

He was last seen about 50 feet from the Canadian shoreline at Table Rock. Witnesses reported hearing a loud bang as he leaped into the air from the jet ski as it went over the edge. Overacker's floating body, clad in a blue life preserver, was recovered from the Niagara River by an employee of the Maid of the Mist. A tape later revealed the parachute, which had been packed into a two-inch diameter open-ended cylinder, had failed to deploy.

The stunter was later pronounced dead by a doctor due to drowning.

The upper portion of the jet ski was destroyed, but the battered hull, with the wording: "Save the Homeless", was intact. The tangled parachute lay strewn across the rocks below the Falls.

Lori Overacker, the stunter's wife, had refused to come to Niagara, fearing the outcome.

Like previous daredevils who made the trip over Niagara Falls, Overacker's name and cause were soon forgotten.

DAREDEVIL No. 16
Kirk Jones, October 20, 2003: Survived

Photo: Niagara Falls Review Archive

Eight years passed before another person would intentionally plummet over Niagara Falls and survive. A 40-year-old Canton, Michigan man, Kirk Jones, went over the Canadian Horseshoe Falls on October 20, 2003, wearing only his jacket and jeans. Miraculously, he survived. He was only the second person to go over Niagara Falls without a barrel, life jacket or other protective device and live to tell about it. One other person cheated the cataract wearing just a life jacket, but seven-year-old Roger Woodward's trip was not planned.

Woodward was a boy thrown into the upper Niagara River in 1960 when a fishing boat he was in capsized. He went over the Falls, was thrown clear of the rocks below and was picked up by the Maid of the Mist. He suffered only minor injuries.

In 2003, emergency crews were called to the brink of the Horseshoe Falls at about 12:45 p.m. when tourists near the brink of the Falls saw Jones go over. Jones was rescued after he swam to shore near the Journey Behind the Falls attraction. He had injured his ribs and lost one shoe in the fall.

In an interview later with ABC's TV's Good Morning America, he said he felt at peace as the swift water pushed him towards the Falls.

"I looked up and the current was ... really spinning fast. I heard the roar get louder and louder. I didn't know exactly when the fall would occur".

He said he felt suction and found himself falling in a wall of water. "I was wondering if this was what it was like to die. It was actually quite beautiful. I had inner peace, despite all the noise and violence".

When he hit the bottom, he realized he was going to survive and he wanted to live.

Jones was unemployed at the time and was said to be depressed. He had been employed for 15 years in a family owned business selling gauging equipment to the auto industry, but it closed, leaving Jones without work. In an exclusive interview with a reporter from the Niagara Falls Review, he is quoted as saying, "It was my full intent to end my life at those Falls. What I did that day was neither heroic nor something that should be emulated in any way, by anyone".

He said that the jump was silly and impulsive and in a second and a half, he was in the water.

In April, 2004, during an interview on Canada AM, Jones put a different spin on the reason why he made the trip: "Well, I have to say it was a challenge to myself. In all my life, I felt I never achieved what I wanted. I was always fascinated by Niagara and I thought once in my life completing a challenge to myself that would no longer (make me fear) the consequences. I would not want people to try what I have done, but sometimes if you believe in yourself you can conquer all obstacles".

In December, 2003, Jones appeared in a Niagara Falls court and was fined $4,500 following his conviction on charges of mischief and performing an illegal stunt. He was also placed on probation for 12 months, with one of the conditions being that he not trespass on lands owned or under control of The Niagara Parks Commission. He was also ordered to pay back $1,408 to the Journey Behind the Falls attraction, which was the money lost when they had to shut down for 45 minutes following the incident.

Jones made several media appearances after his plunge and subsequently joined a circus. Little has been heard of Kirk Jones since the writing of this book.

Acknowledgements

As in previous books, I want to thank those who have gone before me and have recorded the history of these daredevils, especially the reporters for newspaper and magazines.

To Olive Seibel and her late husband George Seibel for their meticulous research of Niagara's history. George Seibel served as historian for both The Niagara Parks Commission and the City of Niagara Falls.

To my son, Michael, who provided contemporary photographs that he has taken of daredevils and to those who have also captured images from the past on film.

I want to thank Lisa Rind, who offered to be the editor of this book. Much appreciated!

I want to give a big round of applause to emergency personnel, especially in the Niagara Parks Police, who have been called upon to put their own lives at risk during the rescue of these daredevils.

Summary of trips Over Niagara to October 20, 2003

No. 1:   October 24, 1901, 63-year-old Annie Edson Taylor in a barrel at about 4:23 p.m. Survived.

No. 2:   July 25, 1911, 54-year-old Bobby Leach in a steel barrel at about 3 p.m. Survived.

No. 3:   July 11, 1920, 58-year-old Charles G. Stephens in an oak barrel at about 8:35 a.m. Died.

No. 4:   July 4, 1928, 36-year-old Jean Albert Lussier in a large rubber ball at about 3:35 p.m. Survived.

No. 5:   July 5, 1930, 46-year-old George A. Stathakis in a huge wooden barrel at about 3:25 p.m. Died.

No. 6:   August 5, 1951, 38-year-old William (Red) Hill Jr., in a contraption made of inner tubes at about 3 p.m. Died.

No. 7:   July 15,1961, 30-year-old William A. Fitzgerald, Ph.D. in a large ball at about 10:56 a.m. Survived.

No. 8:   July 2, 1984, 23-year-old Karel Soucek in a cigar-shaped, plastic barrel at about 9:30 a.m. Survived.

No. 9:   August 18, 1985, 22-year-old Steven Trotter in a barrel made of tractor-trailer inner tubes at about 8 a.m. Survived.

No. 10:   October 5, 1985, 48-year-old John "Dave" Munday in a plastic/aluminum barrel at about 9 a.m. Survived.

No. 11:   September 27, 1989, 42-year-old Peter DeBernardi and 24-year-old Jeffery Petkovich in a mammoth steel barrel at about 5:30 p.m. Survived.

No. 12:   June 5, 1990, 28-year-old Jessie Sharp in a polyethylene kayak at about 1:50 p.m. Died.

No. 13:   September 26, 1993, 56-year-old John "Dave" Munday made a second trip in a converted Canadian Coast Guard diving bell at about 8:35 a.m. Survived.

No. 14:   June 18, 1995, 33-year-old Steven Trotter (his second trip) and 29-year-old Lori Martin in a high-tech plastic barrel at about 9:30 a.m. Survived.

No. 15:   October 1, 1995, 39-year-old Robert Overacker on a jet-ski at about 12:35 p.m. Died.

No. 16:   October 20, 2003, 40-year-old Kirk Jones in just a jacket and jeans at about 12:45 p.m. Survived.

A Word to the Wise

Riding over Niagara Falls in a barrel may seem glamorous.

However, remember these few things:

You can be killed (five have died to date) or become severely disabled.

To perform such a stunt is against the law and fines are steadily increasing. It is likely your vessel will be confiscated.

In many cases, the lives of rescuers are put at risk.

If it's riches you're looking for, forget it. Save the cost of the barrel and invest it in blue chip stocks - your chances are better!